SOUTH AMERICA

Joanne Randolph

raintree

a Capstone company — publishers for children

Raintree is an imprint of Capstone Global Library
Limited, a company incorporated in England and Wales
having its registered office at 264 Banbury Road, Oxford
OX2 7DY – Registered company number: 6695582

www.raintree.co.uk
myorders@raintree.co.uk

Text © Capstone Global Library Limited 2016
The moral rights of the proprietor have been asserted.

Produced for Raintree by Calcium
Edited by Sarah Eason and Katie Woolley
Designed by Paul Myerscough
Illustrations by Moloko88/Shutterstock
Picture research by Sarah Eason
Production by Victoria Fitzgerald
Originated by Capstone Global Library Ltd © 2016

ISBN 978 1 4747 1597 3 (hardback)
19 18 17 16 15
10 9 8 7 6 5 4 3 2 1

ISBN 978 1 4747 1603 1 (paperback)
20 19 18 17 16
10 9 8 7 6 5 4 3 2 1

Printed and bound at Cloc in the UK.

British Library Cataloguing in Publication Data
A full catalogue record for this book is available from the
British Library.

Acknowledgements
We would like to thank the following for permission to
reproduce photographs: Shutterstock: Paulo Afonso 24b,
Alfie Photography 20b, 28l, BMJ 25br, Moritz Buchty 11b,
Rafal Cichawa 13t, 27t, Neale Cousland 26r, Pichugin
Dmitry 1, 4t, 5t, 14b, Andreea Dragomir 19tr, Dirk Ercken
8t, Natali Glado 9b, Guentermanaus 11t, Anton Ivanov
12b, 15r, Jacek Kadaj 17t, Kavram 23t, 29t, Jess Kraft 24t,
Lukasz Kurbiel 17b, Thiago Leite 5r, Alfredo Maiquez 21b,
MP CZ 26l, Nacho Such 19b, Alice Nerr 14–15t, 29br,
Pruit Phatsrivong 10bl, Pyty 4b, 28r, Dr. Morley Read
9t, Elder Vieira Salles 16bl, Serjio74 13b, SNEHIT 6b, 7t,
Sunsinger 18t, 21t, T Photography 7b, Camelia Varsescu
23b, Michael Zysman 27bl; Wikimedia Commons: Paolo
Costa Baldi 23c, Jialiang Gao 11r.

Cover photographs reproduced with permission of:
Shutterstock: Alice Nerr (back cover), Mark Schwettmann
(bottom), Vitmark (top).

Some words are shown in bold, **like this.** You can
find out what they mean by looking in the glossary.

Contents

South America

Patagonia, Argentina

South America is a **continent** in the Western Hemisphere, and most of it lies south of the **equator**. It is a continent with a long and rich history. It has a wide range of **habitats**, including the most **biodiverse** rainforest on the planet and one of the driest places on Earth. Get ready to explore this amazing continent using your best map and maths skills. Let's visit South America!

Pacific Ocean

How to use this book

Look for the "Map-a-stat" and "Do the maths" features and complete the maths challenges. Then look at the answers on pages 28 and 29 to see if your calculations are correct.

Machu Picchu

People have been living in South America for thousands of years, leaving behind cave paintings, tools and ruins that were later discovered by **modern** historians. Perhaps the most famous of South America's ruins are those of Machu Picchu. In AD1450, the Inca people built this great settlement near the city of Cuzco, in modern-day Peru. The Inca had been a **civilization** in the area since the 1200s. Machu Picchu sits 2,350 m (7,710 ft.) above sea level on a mountain that shares its name.

Machu Picchu

Guanaco in Patagonia

Map-a-stat

Machu Picchu is 80 km (50 miles) northwest of Cuzco, which was the capital of the Inca.

Llamas are an iconic South American animal. These camel relatives are used as pack animals in the Andes Mountains.

The animals weigh around 113 kg (250 pounds) and can carry loads of up to 60 kg (132 pounds) for distances of up to 32 km (20 miles).

São Paulo is the largest city in Brazil, which is the largest country in South America.

Atlantic Ocean

São Paulo

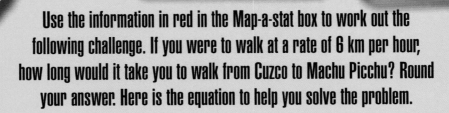

DO THE MATHS!

Use the information in red in the Map-a-stat box to work out the following challenge. If you were to walk at a rate of 6 km per hour, how long would it take you to walk from Cuzco to Machu Picchu? Round your answer. Here is the equation to help you solve the problem.

$$80 \text{ km} \div 6 \text{ km per hour} = ? \text{ hours}$$

Complete the maths challenge, then turn to pages 28—29 to see if your calculation is correct!

A big continent

South America is the fourth-largest continent by area and the fifth-largest based on its population. Its area is 17.9 million sq km (6.9 million sq miles) and it has around 390 million people. The continent is made up of 12 countries. It also has two **territories** that are ruled by other nations. These are the Falkland Islands, controlled by the United Kingdom, and French Guiana, which is under French control.

French Guiana

Venezuela

Colombia

Guyana

Ecuador

Suriname

Brazil

Peru

Bolivia

Chile

Paraguay

Argentina

Uruguay

Falkland Islands

Brazil

Brazil is the largest country within South America. In fact, it takes up about half of the continent's land area and population! By area and number of people, Brazil is the fifth-largest country in the world. More than 203 million people live there. Brazil is home to the Amazon Rainforest, which you will read more about later. The country is also the world's largest producer of coffee.

Rio de Janeiro is the second-largest city in Brazil

Map-a-stat

Brazil takes up 48 per cent of South America's total area.

Brazil has an area of 8.5 million sq km (3.3 million sq miles).

The southern-most inhabited place in South America is Puerto Toro, in Chile. Around 36 people live there.

There are about 22 people per sq km (57 people per sq mile) in South America. In Brazil, there are about 24 people per sq km (62 people per square mile).

These São Paulo favelas (slum areas) fit a lot of people into a very small space

DO THE MATHS!

Use the information in red in the Map-a-stat box to work out the following challenge. How many more people per sq km are there in Brazil compared to the number of people per sq km in South America? Here is the equation to help you solve the problem.

24 people – 22 people = ? more people per sq km

Complete the maths challenge, then turn to pages 28–29 to see if your calculation is correct!

This is a coffee plantation in Alfenas, Brazil

Rainforests

South America is home to many rainforests, including the Amazon Rainforest, the Orinoco Rainforest in the Orinoco River Basin and the Atlantic Rainforest. It is also known for its cloud forests. These are moist forests high in the mountains that often have low clouds for much of the year.

Many **species** of frogs make their home in the Amazon Rainforest

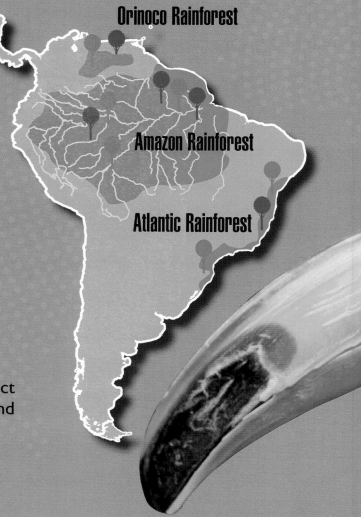

Orinoco Rainforest

Amazon Rainforest

Atlantic Rainforest

The Amazon Rainforest

The Amazon Rainforest is the largest **tropical** rainforest in the world. It covers 6 million sq km (2.3 million sq miles) of land in Brazil, Peru and Colombia. Small parts of it lie in Venezuela, Ecuador, Bolivia, Guyana, Suriname and French Guiana. It is the most biodiverse rainforest in the world, with 16,000 different species of tree, 2.5 million insect species and more than 2,000 species of birds and **mammals**. This is just the tip of the iceberg! The forest also has a huge variety of **reptiles**, **amphibians**, fish and many plant species.

Map-a-stat

One in 10 species in the world lives in the Amazon Rainforest.

Brazil has 60 per cent of the Amazon Rainforest, while Peru has 13 per cent and Colombia has 10 per cent.

Cloud forests in South America tend to be 1,000-3,000 m (3,300-9,850 ft.) above sea level. Most South American cloud forests are along the west coast of the continent.

Ecuadorian cloud forest

Toco toucans are one of the best-known toucan species

DO THE MATHS!

Use the information in red in the Map-a-stat box to work out the following challenge. If Brazil, Peru and Colombia have most of the Amazon Rainforest, what percentage is found in parts of Venezuela, Ecuador, Bolivia, Guyana, Suriname and French Guiana? Here is the equation to help you solve the problem.

$$100 \text{ per cent} - (60 + 13 + 10) = ? \text{ per cent}$$

Complete the maths challenge, then turn to pages 28—29 to see if your calculation is correct!

The Amazon River

Amazon River

Peru

Brazil

The Amazon River is the second-longest river in the world, after Africa's Nile River. It is the greatest in volume, though. The river can be between 4–50 km (2.5–31 miles) wide and is very deep in most areas. The mouth of the river is 64 km (40 miles) wide. Its source is high in the Andes Mountains in Peru. The river empties into the Atlantic Ocean, off the coast of Brazil.

A river full of life

Many species make their homes in and along the Amazon River. In the waters swim giant catfish, piranhas and river dolphins. On the banks are anacondas, jaguars and monkeys. Many people live in small villages or in cities along the Amazon, too. They use the waters to wash, for drinking water, to travel and to catch fish and other animals for food.

The Amazon River dolphin hunts fish in the Amazon River, as well as other South American rivers

Map-a-stat

The Amazon River's length is about 6,437 km (4,000 miles).

At 5,971 km (3,710 miles) long, the Mississippi-Missouri System is the world's fourth-longest river.

Amazon River dolphins often have pink skin and can grow to be 2.4 m (8 ft.) long.

the Amazon River

The source of the Amazon River

This village is on the banks of the Amazon River

DO THE MATHS!

Use the information in red in the Map-a-stat box to work out the following challenge. How much longer is the Amazon River than the Mississippi-Missouri System? Here is the equation to help you solve the problem.

$$6,437 \text{ km} - 5,971 \text{ km} = ? \text{ km longer}$$

Complete the maths challenge, then turn to pages 28—29 to see if your calculation is correct!

Lakes

Most of South America's lakes are found in the Andes or in the foothills of that mountain range. Lake General Carrera, also called Lake Buenos Aires, was formed by glaciers. Shared by Chile and Argentina, the lake is known for its striking blue waters and for two marble cave formations, which were shaped by its waves over thousands of years. Lake Maracaibo is another well-known "lake" in South America. According to some experts, it is not actually a lake but rather a large inlet that connects to the Gulf of Venezuela and the Caribbean Sea.

Lake Maracaibo

Lake Titicaca

Lake General Carrera

Lake Titicaca

Lake Titicaca is the largest lake in South America by volume. It lies on the border of Peru and Bolivia. It has an area of 8,370 sq km (3,232 sq miles). Its deepest parts are 281 m (922 ft.) deep, but on average it is between 140–180 m (460–600 ft.) deep.

These boats and the houses behind them are made out of reeds by the **native people** who live near Lake Titicaca

Map-a-Stat

Lake Maracaibo was formed around 35 million years ago. The long bridge that spans its opening is 8.7 km (5.4 miles) long.

There are around 41 natural islands in Lake Titicaca, some of which have people living on them.

More than 25 rivers flow into Lake Titicaca.

Lake Argentino in the mountains of Argentina is part of Los Glaciares National Park. It is so cold there that icebergs float in the lake's waters!

This woman is walking on the Isla del Sol on Lake Titicaca

Lake General Carrera has beautiful marble caves

DO THE MATHS!

Use the information in red in the Map-a-stat box to work out the following challenge. If you walked at a rate of 3 km per hour across Lake Maracaibo's 8.7 km-long bridge, how long would it take you? Round up your answer. Here is the equation to help you solve the problem.

8.7 km ÷ 3 km per hour
= ? hours

Complete the maths challenge, then turn to pages 28—29 to see if your calculation is correct!

Waterfalls

South America is known for some beautiful waterfalls. Angel Falls, in Venezuela, are two separate falls that, combined, are the world's highest uninterrupted waterfall. The falls are on the Churun River. They have a height of 979 m (3,212 ft.) and their longest drop is 807 m (2,648 ft.).

Iguazu Falls

The Iguazu Falls are shared by Brazil and Argentina. Though they are not the tallest falls in South America, they are an impressive sight. There are many separate waterfalls along the 2.7-km- (1.7 miles) edge, where the upper Iguazu River drops between 60–82 m (197–269 ft.) to the lower Iguazu River. More than half of the river's water falls into a deep U-shaped area called the Devil's Throat.

The Iguazu Falls

Map-a-stat

Kaieteur Falls, in Guyana, is four times higher than the Horseshoe Falls of Niagara Falls, which has a drop of 56 m (185 ft.).

Cuquenán Falls are the second-highest falls in Venezuela, with a single drop of 674 m (2,211 ft.).

Combined, the Gocta Cataracts of Peru have a height of 771 m (2,531 ft.). The local people believe the spirit of a white-haired mermaid protects the falls!

Kaieteur Falls is protected within Kaieteur National Park

Angel Falls lies in a hard-to-reach jungle, but it is still a top tourist stop

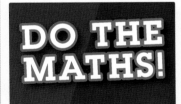

DO THE MATHS!

Use the information in red in the Map-a-stat box to work out the following challenge. If Kaieteur Falls is around four times higher than Horseshoe Falls, how tall is Kaieteur Falls? Here is the equation to help you solve the problem.

$$56 \text{ m} \times 4 = ? \text{ m tall}$$

Complete the maths challenge, then turn to pages 28—29 to see if your calculation is correct!

Coasts

Most people in South America live along the coasts. Much of the central and southern parts of the continent, including Patagonia, have few inhabitants. The west coast of South America has a very dry climate. This is due partly to an ocean **current** off the coast called the Peru Current, which cools the air above it. It is also due to the Andes Mountains, which causes air to lose its moisture as it passes over the mountains. The east coast receives more rainfall than central and southern areas. As a result, the east coast has some **fertile** land.

Itaipuacu is a beautiful beach in Brazil

Sea turtles

South American coasts are important nesting habitats for many different kinds of sea turtles. Leatherbacks, hawksbills and olive ridley turtles are just a few of the species of turtle that haul themselves on to warm beaches, where they dig nests for their eggs. Usually, the hatchlings break free from their eggs. They then make their way towards the ocean, unless they end up as another animal's meal!

Map-a-stat

Sea turtle populations are going down due to many factors, including human action and climate change. The leatherback sea turtle, for example, is now vulnerable. Only a handful of nesting sites are left, including some in French Guiana. Only around 23,000-32,000 adult females remain, and the numbers are dropping quickly.

Patagonia is a region in the southern part of South America. It is shared by Chile and Argentina. Its largest city is Neuquén in Argentina, with a population of more than 345,000 people. The next largest city is Comodoro Rivadavia. It has a population of more than 173,000 people.

The Peruvian coast can be rocky

The coast off the Atacama Desert

DO THE MATHS!

Use the information in red in the Map-a-stat box to work out the following challenge. How many more people are there in the largest Patagonian city than there are in the second-largest one? Here is the equation to help you solve the problem.

345,000 people − 173,000 people = ? more people

Complete the maths challenge, then turn to pages 28—29 to see if your calculation is correct!

Islands

There are hundreds of islands in South America, whether they are off the coasts or inside the continent's many large lakes. Some of these islands are well-known, others are less travelled. One famous island that belongs to Chile is Easter Island, which is known for its giant statues. However, geographically, Easter Island is not actually part of the South American continent.

Houses are built on stilts in Castro, a town on Chiloé Island

Galápagos Islands

Saint Peter and Saint Paul Archipelago

Ecuador

Brazil

Fernando de Noronha

Easter Island

Juan Fernández Islands

Chile

Argentina

Trindade and Martim Vaz

Chiloé Archipelago

Tierra del Fuego

Falkland Islands

So many archipelagos

The Juan Fernández Islands are an **archipelago** of islands that lie 670 km (416 miles) off the coast of Chile. The Chiloé Archipelago is another island chain off the same coast. Tierra del Fuego is made up of many islands and is shared by Chile and Argentina. It has an area of 73,746 sq km (28,473 sq miles). Off the Atlantic Coast, there are islands, too. Brazil **governs** Fernando de Noronha, Trindade and Martim Vaz and the Saint Peter and Saint Paul Archipelago.

Map-a-stat

The Falkland Islands sit off the east coast of Argentina, but they are a territory of the United Kingdom. There are two main islands and 778 smaller ones. The total area of the land is 12,173 sq km (4,700 sq miles).

Easter Island may be part of Chile but it is not close by! It is 3,687 km (2,291 miles) away from Chile.

Trindade and Martim Vaz is a small archipelago with a population of 32 people, although many of these are navy personnel who do not stay on the island permanently. Trindade is the largest island, with an area of 13.5 sq km (5.2 sq miles). The tiny Martim Vaz islets to its east have an area of 0.3 sq km (0.1 sq mile).

Tierra del Fuego

Fernando de Noronha

DO THE MATHS!

Use the information in red in the Map-a-stat box to work out the following challenge. How long would it take you to travel to Easter Island from Chile if you journeyed at a speed of 8 km per hour? Round up your answer. Here is the equation to help you solve the problem.

$$3,687 \text{ km} \div 8 \text{ km per hour} = ? \text{ hours}$$

Complete the maths challenge, then turn to pages 28—29 to see if your calculation is correct!

The Galápagos Islands

The Galápagos Islands are part of Ecuador and lie around 966 km (600 miles) off the coast of that country. The Galápagos is an archipelago. There are 13 main islands and six smaller ones. The largest island is Isabela Island, which has an area of 4,670 sq km (1,803 sq miles).

A wonderworld

The Galápagos Islands are particularly noted for their many unique species of plants and animals, which are found nowhere else on Earth. Marine **iguanas**, Galápagos penguins, flightless **cormorants** and Darwin's finches live on the islands. Crabs and giant tortoises can be found there, too. Amazing underwater populations of sharks, fish and mammals are just a few more of the many creatures that make their homes on and around the islands.

The Galápagos penguin is endangered

Map-a-stat

The Galapágos Islands have a land area of 8,010 sq km (3,093 sq miles), which is spread over 50,100 sq km (19,344 sq miles) of ocean.

There are about 25,000 people living on the Galápagos Islands, and more than 200,000 tourists visit the islands each year.

The Galápagos penguin is the only penguin species that lives north of the equator. There are only 2,000, or fewer, of these penguins left.

Bartolomé Island is one of the islands in the Galápagos archipelago

Marine iguanas sun themselves on the rocks of the Galápagos Islands

DO THE MATHS!

Use the information in red in the Map-a-stat box to work out the following challenge. Over the course of a year, how many more tourists are there in the Galápagos than there are people who live there? Here is the equation to help you solve the problem.

200,000 tourists – 25,000 people = ? more tourists

Complete the maths challenge, then turn to pages 28–29 to see if your calculation is correct!

Mountains

South America is known for the Andes Mountains. This is the longest continental range in the world. It stretches for 8,900 km (5,500 miles) along South America's west coast. The Andes is the highest mountain range outside Asia. The Andes range passes through seven South American countries. These are Venezuela, Colombia, Ecuador, Peru, Bolivia, Chile and Argentina. The range has a lot of high **plateaus**, where many major cities have developed, such as Bogotá, Quito, Mérida and La Paz.

Other highlands

South America also has mountains and highlands outside of the Andes range. The Brazilian Highlands and the Guiana Highlands are two such regions. The tallest peak in the Guiana Highlands is Mount Roraima, which is 2,772 m (9,094 ft.) high. The highest point in the Brazilian Highlands is Pico da Bandeira, which stands at 2,891 m (9,485 ft.).

These mountains are in Torres del Paine in Chilean Patagonia

Mérida

Venezuela

Colombia

Ecuador

Peru

Guiana Highlands

Bogotá

Quito

Brazilian Highlands

La Paz

Bolivia

Andes

Chile

Argentina

Mount Aconcagua

Map-a-stat

The Andes is also home to the world's tallest volcanoes. The tallest volcano of them all is Ojos del Salado, which is 6,893 m (22,615 ft.) high. On the continent, there are many other volcanoes that are more than 6,000 m (19,685 ft.) high.

The Brazilian Highlands take up more than half of Brazil's land area. They cover over 4.5 million sq km (1.7 million sq miles).

At 6,959 m (22,831 ft.) tall, Mount Aconcagua is the tallest peak in the Andes.

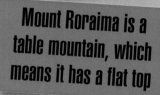

Mount Roraima is a table mountain, which means it has a flat top

Mount Aconcagua is in Argentina and is part of the Andes

DO THE MATHS!

Use the information in red in the Map-a-Stat box to work out the following challenge. How much taller is Mount Aconcagua than Ojos del Salado? Here is the equation to help you solve the problem.

$$6,959 \text{ m} - 6,893 \text{ m} = ? \text{ m taller}$$

Complete the maths challenge, then turn to pages 28—29 to see if your calculation is correct!

Deserts

There are a number of deserts in South America, including the Patagonian Desert, the La Guajira Desert, the Atacama Desert, the Sechura Desert and the Monte Desert.

La Guajira Desert

Sechura Desert

Atacama Desert

Monte Desert

Patagonian Desert

Atacama Desert

The Atacama Desert in Chile is considered one of the driest places on Earth. Scientists believe some parts of the desert's centre have received no rain at all in 400 years! No plants or animals live in these driest regions of the desert. However, more than 1 million people live in the Atacama Desert. Some work at copper mines, some live along the coast. Others work at the Paranal Observatory. There, scientists take advantage of the dry conditions and clear skies to look deep into space using the Very Large Telescope.

Telescopes in the Atacama Desert

Map-a-stat

Most of the La Guajira Desert is in the far north of Colombia but part of it is in Venezuela. The Wayuu people live in the desert. They make a living by diving for pearls, collecting salt and fishing.

The Patagonian Desert in Argentina is the seventh-largest desert in the world. It covers an area of 673,000 sq km (260,000 sq miles). It is a cold desert. Temperatures rarely rise above 12 °C (54 °F), and are usually around 3 °C (37 °F).

The Very Large Telescope has four large telescopes with mirrors that are 8.2 m (27 feet) in diameter. It also has four moveable smaller telescopes with 1.8 m (6 ft) mirrors. These all work together, using computers, to give a picture of space that is 25 times clearer than it would be if seen using one of the telescopes alone.

The Wayuu people make their homes in the La Guajira Desert in Colombia

The Atacama Desert is so dry the earth there is cracked

DO THE MATHS!

Use the information in red in the Map-a-stat box to work out the following challenge. The Sahara Desert has average temperatures that can be as high as 46 °C for many months. How much higher is the Sahara Desert's average temperature than the Patagonian Desert's average temperature? Here is the equation to help you solve the problem.

$$46\,°C - 3\,°C = ?\,°C \text{ hotter}$$

Complete the maths challenge, then turn to pages 28—29 to see if your calculation is correct!

What a continent!

South America is a continent of **extremes**. It has the largest rainforest on Earth, and probably has more species than any other region on the planet. It also has one of the driest places on Earth. It has warm, tropical beaches and bustling cities. It has glaciers and tiny villages where people live much as they did hundreds of years ago.

People in Bolivia and other South American countries raise llamas for wool and other uses

Women in Peru are known for their weaving and the beautiful cloth that they make

Economy and industry

South America has a growing **economy**. One of its main industries is agriculture. In tropical areas, nuts, coffee and **cacao** are some of the crops grown. In the cooler areas, corn and soybeans are big money-making crops. Because South America has a lot of **grasslands**, including the Pampas, it also has a lot of **livestock**. Brazil is the world's third-largest producer of beef. Even in the drier climates of South America, potatoes, **quinoa** and rice are grown. Aside from agriculture, forestry, fishing and mining are major industries. South America has many important metals, and is also a producer of natural gas and oil.

Map-a-stat

More than one-third of the world's copper is found in South America, in Peru and Chile. Chile is the world's largest exporter of copper.

Venezuela exports a lot of oil and gas. This business makes up one-fifth of the country's economy.

São Paulo, Brazil, is the continent's largest city. It has a population of more than 11 million people. The São Paulo metropolitan area, which includes the surrounding cities and towns, has a population of nearly 20 million people.

People sell fruit and vegetables at this market in Ecuador

The woolly monkey is just one of the many amazing creatures found in South America

DO THE MATHS!

Use the information in red in the Map-a-stat box to work out the following challenge. What is the difference between the number of people who live in São Paulo city and those who live in the metropolitan area? Here is the equation to help you solve the problem.

20,000,000 people –
11,000,000 people
= ? people

Complete the maths challenge, then turn to pages 28—29 to see if your calculation is correct!

Maths challenge answers

You have made it through the mathalon!
How did your maths skills measure up?
Check your answers below.

Page 5

$80 \text{ km} \div 6 \text{ km per hour}$
$= 13 \text{ hours}$

Page 7

24 people – 22 people
= 2 more people per sq km

Page 9

100 per cent – (60 + 13 + 10)
= 17 per cent

Page 11

$6{,}437 - 5{,}971 \text{ km}$
$= 466 \text{ km longer}$

Page 13

$8.7 \text{ km} \div 3 \text{ km per}$
hour = about 3 hours

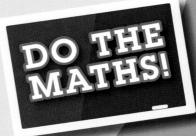

Page 15

56 m x 4 = 224 m tall

Page 17

345,000 people – 173,000 people
= 172,000 more people

Page 19

3,687 km ÷ 8 km per hour = about 461 hours

Page 21

200,000 tourists – 25,000 people = 175,000 more tourists

Page 23

6,959 m – 6,893 m
= 66 m taller

DO THE MATHS!

Page 25

46 °C – 3 °C = 43 °C hotter

Page 27

20,000,000 people –
11,000,000 people
= 9,000,000 people

Glossary

amphibian cold-blooded animal that spends part of its life in water and part on land

archipelago group of islands

biodiverse having a large number of different types of living thing in a certain habitat

cacao bean-like seed from which cocoa, or chocolate, is made

civilization people who have an organized society

climate change change in Earth's overall climate, thought to be brought about by human action, such as the burning of coal and gas

continent one of Earth's seven large landmasses

cormorant type of seabird

current part of a larger mass of water or air that flows in one direction

economy system of how money is made and used within a particular region or country

equator imaginary line around the middle of Earth

exporter person, organization or country that sells goods to another country

extreme great difference

fertile describes ground that is rich and able to produce crops and other plants

glacier large mass of ice that moves down a mountain or along a valley

govern organize and run an area and its people

grassland large area of land covered by grass

habitat surrounding area where animals or plants naturally live

iconic something that is recognized as being important to a place or a people, and representative of them

iguana type of large lizard that often has a ridge of spines along its back

inhabited lived in. An inhabited place is an area in which people live.

islet very small island

livestock farm animals, such as cattle and sheep, kept for their meat, wool or skin

mammal animal that has warm blood and often fur. Most mammals give birth to live young and feed their babies with milk from their bodies.

modern recent, not ancient. Also means using the most up-to-date ideas or ways of doing things.

native people people who are born in a place and whose ancestors lived there

plateau large, flat area that is at a higher altitude than the surrounding region

protect keep from harm

quinoa grain crop that is rich in protein

reptile animal that has scales covering its body and that uses the sun to control its body temperature

species single kind of living thing. All people are one species.

territory particular area of land that belongs to and is controlled by a country

tropical having to do with the warm parts of Earth that are near the equator

Find out more

Books

Brazil (Countries in Our World), Edward Parker
(Franklin Watts, 2012)

Riding the Americas: The Boy Who Biked the World, Alastair Humphreys
(Eye Books, 2014)

South America: Everything You Ever Wanted to Know (Not for Parents)
(Lonely Planet, 2014)

South America (Introducing Continents), Anita Ganeri
(Raintree, 2014)

South America (Rookie Read-About Geography), Rebecca Hirsch
(Scholastic, 2012)

Websites

Find out more about South America at:
www.ducksters.com/geography/southamerica.php

Read even more information about South America at:
kids.britannica.com/comptons/article-9277149/
   South-America

Discover more facts about South America at:
www.timeforkids.com/around-the-world

Index